JAKARTA EE DEPENDENCY INJECTION FOR JAVA DEVELOPERS

Luqman Saeed

A PRACTICAL GUIDE TO DEPENDENCY INJECTION ON THE JAKARTA EE (FORMERLY JAVA EE) PLATFORM

TABLE OF CONTENTS

http://pedanticacademy.com

PREFACE

Thank you for picking up Jakarta EE Dependency Injection for Java Developers. I wrote this book as a response to the lack of easy to understand books on using the compelling and intuitive Contexts and Dependency Injection API on the Jakarta EE (formerly Java EE) platform.

This book covers the very essentials of the CDI API and aims at explaining the various constructs in a way that is easy to understand and relate to. The ultimate goal is to help you, the everyday Java developer, write better code. Throughout the book, you will be working on a simple restaurant application, seeing when and how the various CDI API constructs can be used.

WHAT DO I NEED TO KNOW
TO USE THIS BOOK?

Ideally, you should be a Java developer who is comfortable with Java SE before starting with this book. Knowing a bit of Java EE or Spring should help you pick up the concepts faster but isn't required. You should also have the JDK installed on your machine.

WHAT DOES THE BOOK COVER?

The book starts with the theory of Java EE, its evolution to present-day Jakarta EE, and proceeds to cover CDI starting with how to activate it explicitly. The discussion then builds upon the concept of CDI beans and discusses the various types. You will then learn about CDI contexts and injection points. The book then introduces CDI qualifiers, producers, interceptors and finally CDI events.

WHAT WILL I LEARN AT THE END?

Jakarta EE Dependency Injection for Java Developers is a very concise book that covers only what matters. Your time is important, so I only selected topics that I use personally in my day to day coding. There's no point in loading the book with topics you will only use sparingly. So this book should be straightforward to consume over a weekend.

At the end of this book, you will develop a firm grasp of the Contexts and Dependency Injection API, what it is, when to use it and how to write better, readable and maintainable code with it.

WHERE IS THE SOURCE CODE?

The entire code for the book is available on GitHub. The project is built with the Maven dependency management tool and should work in any IDE that supports maven. If you don't have Maven installed, you can follow this guide to install it on your machine. It is available for all OS out there. I highly encourage you to clone the code to your local machine to follow along with the book.

The project object model (pom.xml) file contains the Payara Micro maven plugin that you can use to run the code sample. Change to the project directory and issue the command

```
mvn package payara-micro:start
```

To get the Async CDI events running, you will need to download the Payara Server Full Stream and follow this video to run the cloned code.

HOW DO I REACH YOU?

Writing a book is a tedious task, and as such, despite best efforts, there may be errors that escape through quality checks. I take full responsibility for all of them.

Should you encounter any such errors, need help with anything in this book, or would like to hang out for coffee, please don't hesitate to reach out to me personally.

Once again, thank you for picking up this book, I hope you write better code after reading it. Let's get started.

Luqman Saeed
25th May, 2019.

To my lovely wife, Ayisha. Thank you for your patience. To my closest friend and son, Sheikh Husary, thank you for the companionship.

WHAT IS JAVA EE?

The Java Enterprise Edition, formerly known as J2EE, at its core, is just a collection of *abstract, standardized specifications* that prescribes solutions to commonly faced challenges in software development.

It's important to note the words abstract in the above definition. This means that Java EE is just a set interfaces and contracts that provides a public facing API for developers.

These abstract specs are also said to be standardized. What does this also mean? It means that the entire collection of Java EE APIs are published according to well-defined criteria set by experts in the subject field of the API[1].

By standardized, it also means that every Java EE API has gone through the rigorous process of the Java Community Process's Java spec Request program. The result of this process is a set of APIs that are industry tried and tested and are deemed to be here to stay.

However, remember we said Java EE is abstract right? Well even though you will generally code against the Java EE APIs in the *javax.** packages, you can't run your application on Java EE per SE.

So How Do I Run a Java EE App?
To run a Java EE application, you will need a concrete implementation of the Java EE spec. Remember we said they're abstract? The official name given to the concrete implementation of Java EE is Application Server. I bet you've heard that before right?

An Application Server is basically a concrete implementation of the entire Java EE abstract specs. This means that you run your application code using Java EE API implementations on an Application Server.

There are many application servers out there including Payara Server, Apache TomEE, JBoss Wildfly, IBM OpenLiberty among others.

WHAT IS A JAVA SPECIFICATION REQUEST (JSR)?

At its core, a Java Specification Request is a formal, open standard document proposal that is made by an individual or organization to the Java Community Process (JCP)[2], that contains proposed changes, additions and improvements to the Java technology platform.

Many essential points could be gleaned from the above definition. First is that a JSR is a formal document. What this means is that a JSR or a request for adding to the Java technology group must take a certain predefined format. A format defined by the JCP.

Also, a JSR is an open standard document. What this means again, is that a JSR is a document that conforms to certain laid down rules and regulations regarding its distribution and contributions to it. It also means that whatever is contained in the JSR is easily accessible to anyone interested in assessing it.

Flowing from our definition of a Java Specification Request is that a JSR can be made by either an individual or organization. Any member of the JCP can make a JSR. JCP membership is opened to the public; free for individuals as well. So what this also means is that one cannot make a request to the JCP without being a member of the organization.

Then finally, a JSR is a document that proposes changes, additions and improvements to the Java technology platform. This means that every JSR is an addition of new features or bug fixes or general improvements, in one way or the other, to the Java technology stack.

Every major API available on Java EE is actually a JSR specification that has gone through the process of being approved by the JCP. All JSRs have a process they have to go through to be approved by the JCP.

Once a JSR is approved by the JCP, it becomes a part of the Java stack and can be safely used in production. The JSR process ensures that only well tested technologies are made a part of the Java stack, preventing unnecessary bloat to the platform in the form of adding fad technologies.

The JSR process also ensures that APIs are carefully crafted in such a way to preserve backward compatibility. If there is one thing Java is known for, it's backward compatibility, and the JSR process ensures this crucial Java feature is maintained.

As a JSR is just an abstract specification, it needs some form of implementation to be any useful. That is where the concept of reference implementation comes in.

WHAT IS A REFERENCE IMPLEMENTATION?

In the previous chapter, we looked at what a JSR is. We did say that a JSR is an abstract request to the JCP that contains proposed additions to the Java technology platform.

Because it is abstract, you cannot run it. A JSR needs to have some form of implementation, or concrete realization to be useful to us end developers. So that is where the concept of Reference Implementation comes in.

Every JSR must have a reference implementation, which is a concrete implementation of the specification contained in the JSR document. This is a requirement of the JCP. Every single JSR has a reference implementation that is freely available and mostly bundled with the application servers.

A JSR also has TCK or Technology Compatibility Kit which is "a suite of tests that at least nominally checks a particular alleged implementation of a Java Specification Request (JSR) for compliance."[3]

A TCK is used to test a JSR implementation for compliance with the spec. This is part of why Java EE is said to be a standardized set of specifications.

This rigorous process also ensures the quality of the APIs that are derived from the JSR document. Some popular reference implementations (RIs) of some JSRs are

- . JSR 380 (Bean Validation 2.0) – Hibernate Validator 6
- . JSR 367 (JSON-B Binding) – Eclipse Yasson 1.0
- . JSR 370 (JAX-RS 2.1) – Jersey
- . JSR 365 (CDI 2.0) – WELD 3.0

These are some of the new and popular JSRs and their respective reference implementations. Also, most of these reference implementations are bundled with applications servers, which is the subject of the next chapter.

WHAT IS AN APPLICATION SERVER?

In the previous chapter, we talked about what a JSR reference implementation is. Also in our definition of Java EE, we did mention that it is a collection of abstract specifications. Now Java EE itself, is a Java Specification Request.

Better still, Java EE is what is termed an umbrella JSR in that it encapsulates some JSRs. So Java EE 7 for instance, is JSR 342. Java EE 8 is JSR 366. So Java EE itself is a JSR that goes through the JCP JSR process and is subject to the requirements of every JSR.

Flowing from the above, and remember we did say that the JSR process requires every JSR to have a reference implementation, this means Java EE as an umbrella JSR must also have a reference implementation.

So the implementation of the umbrella JSR or Java EE is what is commonly referred to as an application server. An app server is a concrete implementation of the Java EE spec that you can actually run your code on. The reference implementation of Java EE is the Glassfish Application Server.

An application server generally abstracts you the developer away from a lot of mundane stuff that you would have had to manage on your own, like data-source pooling, caching, clustering, and other overheads.

The application server must also pass the TCK to be fully certified as being compliant with a given umbrella JSR. An app server is also the basis for the portability of Java EE. As a developer, you generally are encouraged to code against the javax.* packages, which are the standard Java EE packages.

Now because an app server is subject to a standard, using the Java EE package will mean you can swap out application servers and your code will generally run with little to no modifications. This is compelling if you think about it.

How so? Because for starters, no single application vendor can lock you in. Because you can swap out application servers, theoretically you could change vendors at any time should you be dissatisfied with one vendor.

There are many application vendors out there, some free, some costly. Popular among the open source ones is Payara Server, a Glassfish derived, fully patched, application server that is freely available for download.

So Java EE is an abstract spec and its concrete realization or implementation is what is called an application server. So as a JSR, the required reference implementation of Java EE is the Glassfish application server.

WHAT IS JAKARTA EE?

We have looked at what Java EE is. We've seen what an application server is and how it relates to the term Java EE. However, what is Jakarta EE?

Jakarta EE is the new Java EE. Back in 2017, Oracle, which was the owner of the Java EE technology stack decided to open the platform further to the wider community. In the process, the entire Java EE platform had to be moved to a non-profit, community oriented foundation.

The Java EE community voted and chose the Eclipse Foundation. So, Java EE was moved to the Eclipse Foundation. Due to legal issues, the name of the platform had to be changed to something else from its original Java EE. Again the community made suggestions and eventually the name Jakarta EE won.

With a renewed goal of aligning the former Java EE platform to more modern software development paradigms, the Eclipse Foundation is seeking to position Jakarta EE as a modern, cloud native, agile software development platform.

One of the criticisms levelled against Java EE was that it was too slow to evolve. The software development landscape moved faster than the platform could keep up. In light of such valid concerns, the Eclipse Foundation through the Jakarta EE working group developed the following guiding principles for Jakarta EE

- . deliver more frequent releases
- . lower barriers to participation
- . develop the community
- . manage the Jakarta EE brand on behalf of the community

Initially Jakarta EE is the exact equivalent to the Java EE 8 platform. All of the specifications, reference implementations (RIs), and technology compatibility kits (TCKs) that comprised Java EE 8 have been transferred to the Eclipse Foundation[4]. This means that the former Java EE 8 release is the foundation of the new cloud native Jakarta EE.

In previous chapters, we had discussed how Java EE was evolved through the concept of Java Specification Requests (JSRs) through the Java Community Process (JCP). However, how will Jakarta EE be evolved at the Eclipse Foundation? Alternatively, how is the Jakarta EE governance model different from that of Java EE?

The main difference is that the Jakarta EE governance model is now community-based, multi-vendor, and open to participation and contribution by the enterprise consumers of these technologies. The Eclipse Foundation will ensure that the new specifications and development processes for

Jakarta EE will be open, vendor-neutral, and provide a level playing field for all participants.

The Java Community Process (JCP) will be replaced by the Eclipse Foundation Specification Process (EFSP). How is it different from the JCP?

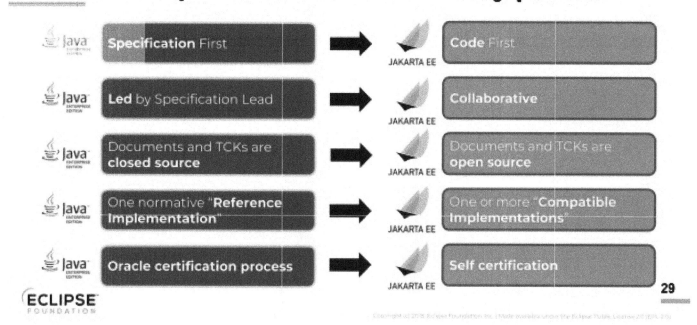

Image Credit

Code first approach - The most vital difference between the JCP and EFSP is that specifications are going to be developed through a code first approach. In the JCP, the specification is developed, followed by the reference implementation. In the EFSP however, there will be hands-on coding and experimenting first to be sure something is worthy of being included in a specification document.

The other differences all have more openness on the side of the EFSP than on the erstwhile JCP process. This is a good thing. It means you as a developer can feel safe in using the Jakarta EE platform for your applications knowing that it is a fully open platform run by a non-profit organization, with a broader participation by the entire Java community. Microsoft and Pivotal (the company behind the Spring Framework) are all members of the Jakarta EE community.

With regards to releases, the first release of the umbrella specification under Eclipse Foundation is Glassfish 5.1, which is a Java EE 8 compatible release. Remember in the Reference Implementation chapter, we stated that the Glassfish application server is the reference implementation of the Java EE umbrella JSR. The Foundation plans to release a Glassfish version 5.2 in the first half of 2019, which is expected to be Jakarta EE 8 compatible.

The future for you as a Jakarta EE developer is inspiring. There is a lot of community interest in moving the entire Jakarta EE platform forward, aiming to make it the most reliable, cloud native, enterprise Java development platform of choice for modern software development paradigms. Wouldn't you want to master this exciting platform?

WHY JAKARTA EE?

As a Java developer, you are spoilt for choice when it comes to frameworks and platforms for software development. A question you might be asking yourself is why should I choose Jakarta EE as my primary software development platform? What makes it a better choice?

There are number of reasons to at least give Jakarta EE a try, key among them being

1. Standardization

2. Openness

3. Stability

4. Ease of development

5. Portability

6. Pick and choose - tank or pistol

7. Amazing documentation

Standardization

Every single JSR has gone through a rigorous process of both public and the JSR Expert Group scrutiny before finally voted on by the JCP EC, for all Java EE APIs. Every JSR weighed in terms of backward compatibility, benefit to the Java platform as a whole etc. Painstaking JSR approval process ensured every feature is accepted based on certain well-defined technical criteria. Similarly, every API of the new Jakarta EE platform will go through a well-defined specification process to ensure whatever API is included in the platform is going to be there for the long haul.

Openness

As discussed earlier, new Jakarta EE specifications are going to be developed in a code first approach through the Eclipse Foundation Specification Process. The EFSP is an open process that anyone can be a part of. The entire speechification process is developed in the open.

Openness

Jakarta EE being a standard means the Eclipse Foundation will only accept and standardize industry tried and tested technology. For long-lived apps that will require maintenance, no room for using fad tech that will vanish tomorrow. Every Jakarta EE technology is industry tried and tested and here for the long haul.

Ease of Development

Jakarta EE development is effortless. All that's needed is an application server or Jakarta EE compliant runtime and one maven dependency. Minimal configuration. Convention over configuration. No XML hell. Sensible defaults. Ex- EJBs transactional by default, default data-source, CDI enabled by default.

```
1 <dependency>
2   <groupId>javax</groupId>
3   <artifactId>javaee-api</artifactId>
4   <version>8.0</version>
5   <scope>provided</scope>
6 </dependency>
7
```

The above code snippet is the only dependency you need to have the entire Jakarta EE platform available at your fingertips. Moreover, because you're abstracted from the implementation of the standard, you only package your application with your code and other third-party libraries used. Your chosen application server will provide the implementation and all the other heavy lifting required to run an application.

Portability
Jakarta EE as a standard means that your application should work with minimal to no configuration across various implementations of the standard, as long as you the developer did code against the standard. This is compelling because you don't get locked into any given Jakarta EE application runtime vendor. Your code is portable across various application servers as long as you use the standard Jakarta EE APIs.

Pick and choose - tank or pistol
Jakarta EE is a huge platform that may appear intimidating. But you can pick and choose whatever API in the group your application requires. You can use the platform as a tank or pistol - you decide. All the various APIs are integrated as a whole if you choose to use Jakarta EE as a tank, or can stand alone individually if you choose to nitpick. Also, as the application server provides the runtime implementation, whether you choose to use the entire platform or just a select APIs, you still ship your application with just your code. Either way, your application is always shipped as a lightweight bundle.

Java EE 8

Batch	Dependency Injection	JACC	JAXR	JSTL	Management
Bean Validation	Deployment	JASPIC	JMS	JTA	Servlet
CDI	EJB	JAX-RPC	JSF	JPA	Web Services
Common Annotations	EL	JAX-RS	JSON-P	JavaMail	Web Services Metadata
Concurrency EE	Interceptors	JAX-WS	JSP	Managed Beans	WebSocket
Connector	JSP Debugging	JAXB			
JSON-B	Security				

Image Credit

Amazing documentation

Jakarta EE is a well organized community project that has an amazing amount of documentation. Chief among this is the Java EE Tutorials[4], the official Java EE handbook. There are also lots of community and corporate organized conferences like Devoxx and Oracle CodeOne that place a lot of emphasis on server side Java development. There are also books written by individual developers like this one you are reading, all focused on helping you become a well grounded enterprise Java software developer.

The above points are just a few reasons why you should give Jakarta EE a try. I know in the J2EE days, the platform was a unwieldy thing for a lot of people. However, today, Jakarta EE is a nimble, elegant, deceptively simple but compelling software development platform, as you will be seeing in the second part of this book.

JAKARTA EE AND THE SPRING FRAMEWORK

A book on Jakarta EE will not be complete without a discussion about the Spring Framework. So what is the Spring Framework?

The Spring Framework is an alternative server side software development platform for the JVM that runs on a servlet container. It used to be Java based but you can now develop Spring apps with some other JVM based languages like Kotlin. Spring Framework came about because of the frustrations developers faced using the earlier versions of Java EE, then called J2EE.

Rod Johnson[5] started the project as an alternative platform that was more developer friendly and less arcane than then J2EE. In the beginning, the Spring Framework was just an inversion of control (dependency injection) framework. It soon became very popular and has since grown to become a full stack alternative to Jakarta EE. The Spring Framework intellectual property is owned by Pivotal Inc.

However, as Spring was growing, developers started experiencing pain points that caused them lots of frustrations with the platform[6]. At the same time that Spring was enjoying all the popularity, then Java EE was also evolving with all the feedback it was getting.

The release of Java EE 7 marked a milestone in the history of the platform, because it had almost caught up with the Spring Framework in terms of developer productivity but had managed to avoid the pitfalls. Java EE releases have been heavily influenced by the Spring Framework.

Today, Spring as a platform has the Spring Boot framework, a framework I like to call "Little Java EE for Spring". Spring Boot has been influenced by Java EE's convention over configuration and sensible default philosphy. Both platforms have been very influential over the other.

As a Java developer, you have the choice of using Jakarta EE or the Spring Framework. Neither, for me, is really superior over the other. Both platforms have their strengths and weaknesses. Naturally as the author of a Jakarta EE book, I choose Jakarta EE, but that is because I am excited about its future as an Eclipse Foundation community project, I feel effective using it and I find it easy to learn and teach it.

You should choose a platform based on its technical merits to you, how easy you can maintain your apps, how much you value backwards compatibility and other such metrics. My opinion about the whole Spring vs Java EE flame wars is that it's just not worth it. They are both excellent platforms that cater to different kinds of developers. Pivotal, the company behind the Spring Framework is now a member of the Jakarta EE community.

Spring Framework vs Java EE can be rephrased as Spring Framework and Jakarta EE. You as a developer should pick what is right in your context. As you are reading this book, I am certain you have already decided which you want to go with.

THE CONTEXTS AND DEPENDENCY INJECTION (CDI) API

Dependency injection is a way of developing software such that various components are related in a very loosely coupled way. In most software applications, there is always some form of dependency between the various bits and pieces.

Take a restaurant application for instance, you might have a component that handles taking orders, another for sending a message to the kitchen, yet another for checking available ingredients for a given meal, and maybe one or two for calculating the total bill.

These are all various components that need to depend on each other to fulfil the duty of a running a restaurant. However, creating and managing this interdependency can be a difficult task. You will need to create individual dependencies for each component, and at times, think of the contexts within which you want a specific dependency to exist.

This is where the concept of dependency injection comes in. With DI, your various components simply declare a dependency on other components and leave the creation, management and destruction of these dependencies to an external mechanism. In short, you invert control in your application. Components simply request for a dependency and some black box makes that dependency available. That black box is generally referred to as an inversion of control (IoC) container.

Dependency injection is a specific type of IoC "which concerns itself with decoupling dependencies between high-level and low-level layers through shared abstractions."[7] Contexts and Dependency Injection (CDI) is an implementation of the DI principle

CDI ACTIVATION

On the Jakarta EE platform, the API that helps you glue together the disparate components of your application code is the Contexts and Dependency Injection (CDI) API. In its version 2.0, CDI is activated by default in Jakarta EE with the discovery mode set to annotated.

What the default activation scope means is that only beans (or Java classes) annotated with CDI annotations or CDI recognized annotations are eligible for injection. The default CDI config file, a small XML file called beans.xml in the /webapp/WEB-INF folder looks as shown below

```xml
<?xml version="1.0" encoding="UTF-8"?>
<beans xmlns="http://xmlns.jcp.org/xml/ns/javaee"
    xmlns:xsi="http://www.w3.org/2001/XMLSchema-instance"
    xsi:schemaLocation="http://xmlns.jcp.org/xml/ns/javaee
http://xmlns.jcp.org/xml/ns/javaee/beans_1_1.xsd"
    bean-discovery-mode="annotated">
</beans>
```

Line 5 in the above image is the default bean discovery
mode, where bean discovery mode is simply the scanning mechanism for identifying beans that are eligible to be managed by the CDI container. Annotated means only classes with bean defining annotations will be discovered during scanning.

This implies the following bean will be scanned at application boot time.

```java
1 @ApplicationScoped
2 public class TableService {
3
4     private final Collection<TableNum> assignedTables = new HashSet<>
5 ();
6
7     public boolean assignTable(TableNum tableNum) {
8         return assignedTables.add(tableNum);
9     }
10
11    public boolean checkTableAvailability(TableNum tableNum) {
12        return assignedTables.contains(tableNum);
13    }
14 }
```

However, this class will not be scanned for lack of a bean defining annotation.

```java
1
2 public class TableService {
3
4     private final Collection<TableNum> assignedTables = new HashSet<>
5 ();
6
7     public boolean assignTable(TableNum tableNum) {
8         return assignedTables.add(tableNum);
9     }
10
11    public boolean checkTableAvailability(TableNum tableNum) {
12        return assignedTables.contains(tableNum);
13    }
14 }
```

Do note that this is the kind of beans.xml file that kicks in in the absence of an explicitly created one.

Using the CDI API with the default bean discovery mode set to annotated isn't quite fun, however. To utilize the power of Jakarta EE dependency injection fully, you would want to set the bean discovery mode to All.

```xml
1 <?xml version="1.0" encoding="UTF-8"?>
2 <beans xmlns="http://xmlns.jcp.org/xml/ns/javaee"
3     xmlns:xsi="http://www.w3.org/2001/XMLSchema-instance"
4     xsi:schemaLocation="http://xmlns.jcp.org/xml/ns/javaee
  http://xmlns.jcp.org/xml/ns/javaee/beans_1_1.xsd"
5     bean-discovery-mode="all">
6 </beans>
```

Setting the bean discovery mode to all as seen in Line 5 of the above image, means all classes will be discovered during scanning by the CDI container at application startup. So, whether a bean has a CDI annotation or not, as long as it's in the same archive (a bundle of a given Jakarta EE app), it will be discovered. This is what you will find in a lot of Jakarta EE code out there. It's also my preferred and recommended mode.

THE CDI CONTAINER

The word container is most often associated with dependency injections. So what is the CDI container? It's the heartbeat of your CDI code. It validates your CDI code at application startup and ensures that all your CDI code is valid. It's very rare getting a CDI runtime error.

The CDI container is responsible for creating contextual instances of your beans, adding relevant CDI magic to those created instances, assigning them to relevant contexts and finally destroying those instances when the contexts they're bound to get destroyed.

You can think of the CDI container as a black box that only appears to answer your requests and disappears into the shadows when not needed. You as a developer will mostly not need to think much about the CDI container however, you just have to know it's there in the background, and ready to answer your requests.

CDI BEANS VS CONTEXTUAL INSTANCES

Up to this point in the book, we have been using the term beans and contextual instances quite freely, without defining what they mean. So, what exactly is meant by beans?

The CDI spec defines beans as a source of contextual objects which define application state and/or logic. These objects are called contextual instances of the bean.[8] All that means is that a bean is the Java class that you, as a developer, write.

You implement your bean logic in Java code and then use relevant CDI annotations to provide it with attributes that you would want the bean's contextual instance to posses. It's the template from which instances can be created and injected in the dependency injection process. The CDI container discovers your beans at application startup by scanning your application archive.

A bean then is just a collection of metadata associated with your Java code, from which the container creates objects to satisfy a given dependency injection request. That CDI created object from your bean is what is called a contextual instance.

The set of attributes that you can give your beans are Qualifiers, Scopes, Alternatives and Name. We will be discussing these attributes throughout the rest of this chapter.

CREATING AND USING BEANS

As stated earlier, a CDI bean is just a regular Java class with CDI metadata applied in the form of annotations. Take a look at the most basic CDI bean below.

```
1
2  public class TableService {
3
4      private final Collection<TableNum> assignedTables = new HashSet<>
5  ();
6
7      public boolean assignTable(TableNum tableNum) {
8          return assignedTables.add(tableNum);
9      }
10
11     public boolean checkTableAvailability(TableNum tableNum) {
12         return assignedTables.contains(tableNum);
13     }
14 }
```

In the above code, we have a very boring plain old Java object with no explicit CDI annotations called TableService. This class is a valid CDI bean because we have set our CDI discovery mode to all. This means we can request for contextual instances of this bean from the CDI container, and it will honor our request.

However, in our restaurant application, we want to have only one instance of the Table Service responsible for checking the availability and assignment of tables to guests. In this case, we need to modify our bean - or template - from which the only-one-instance contextual instance will be created.

@APPLICATIONSCOPED

To do this, we need to use the @ApplicationScoped[9] annotation to define a metadata on the bean.

```
1  @ApplicationScoped
2  public class TableService {
3
4      private final Collection<TableNum> assignedTables = new HashSet<>
5  ();
6
7      public boolean assignTable(TableNum tableNum) {
8          return assignedTables.add(tableNum);
9      }
10
11     public boolean checkTableAvailability(TableNum tableNum) {
12         return assignedTables.contains(tableNum);
13     }
14 }
```

The code above shows our TableService class now bearing an explicit bean defining annotation called @ApplicationScoped. This annotation tells the CDI container to put the contextual instance of this bean in a specific, well defined scope, or context, called application.

Scopes, or contexts, are a way of telling the CDI container how you want it to manage the life cycle of your contextual instances. Instances you request from the CDI container will be placed in relevant contexts, that are determined by either the explicit metadata you the developer provide along with your bean code, or one that the CDI container defaults to.

So, what does the application scope or context mean? It means that for our TableService, we only want to have one contextual instance for the entire application. Every single request for a TableService from the CDI container will be serviced with the same contextual instance. Think of application scoped as shared state contextual instance across the lifetime of the deployed application.

The good thing about CDI scopes is that they are well defined. You can predict when an instance will be existence and when it will be destroyed. You can use this knowledge to craft powerful dependency graphs in your application. So what are the other available scopes aside from @Application-

Scoped?

Other CDI Scopes

@REQUESTSCOPED[10]

This scope binds a contextual instance to a context that is created and destroyed for every request. In a typical HTTP environment, every HTTP request will result in the creation of a new contextual instance and its destruction at the end of the request. In a non-HTTP environment, a bean annotated with @RequestScoped will have its contextual instances always created and destroyed for every given request.

In our restaurant application, we could have a class that handles searching for orders. This class typically should be request scoped so we have different instances for each request for a search. You would want a clean slate for every search request.

```java
1 @RequestScoped
2 public class SearchService {
3
4
5     private final Collection<Order> searchResults = new HashSet<>();
6     public Collection<Order> searchOrders(String reqQueryString, String... optionalQueryStrings) {
7         //perform search in datastore and put results in searchResults
8
9         return searchResults;
10    }
11 }
12
```

In the above code, we have a class named SearchService that is annotated with @RequestScoped on line 1. This explicitly tells the CDI container to bind every instance of this bean to a scope called request. For every request for a contextual instance of this bean, a new instance will be created and put in a new scope. So multiple requests by a given user will result in new instances for each request.

@SESSIONSCOPED[11]

This scope binds instances of an annotated bean to a context that spans a given user session. Think of a session context as a guard that follows a user around an application as long as they are interacting with the application. The session scope is more or less the HTTP session for a given user.

In our application, we could have a bean that tracks a logged in user, where that logged in user could be the restaurant manager or cashier.

```
1 @SessionScoped
2 public class UserSession implements Serializable {
3
4     private String userName;
5     private LocalDateTime loggedInTime;
6     private LocalDateTime loggedOutTime;
7
8 }
```

In the above code, we have a bean named UserSession that is annotated with @SessionScoped on line 1. This tells the CDI container to create an instance of this class per user per session. So every user will have one contextual instance of this class for each session. Multiple requests for an instance of this class by a user in the same session will result in the same contextual instance being supplied.

Of note in this bean declaration is that it implements the Serializable interface as shown on line 2. This is good practice because the contextual instance might get passivated - or saved - by the container to save system resources when not in use. So it's good practice to mark it with the serializable interface.

@CONVERSATIONSCOPED[12]

Conversation scoped beans are used to perform tasks that transcend one request but are shorter than a session. A typical example of @ConversationScoped use case is placing an order. Order items are held in a cart from the time a user starts picking items and are finally emptied when the user checks out. In between, the user might navigate across multiple ages of the application.

You can use conversation scoped beans to manage such a conversation between the user and your application without having to necessarily keep the bean alive once the user gets done with the shopping.

Conversation scoped beans are by default in a transient state, that is, they're eligible to be destroyed at any time. Unlike the other scopes you've seen so far, you will have to initiate a bean into a conversation state manually. How do you do that? Back to our restaurant application, we could have a bean annotated @ConversationScoped that is used to place an order in the system.

```java
1  @ConversationScoped
2  public class OrderService implements Serializable {
3
4      @Inject
5      Conversation conversation;
6
7      public void beginOrderProcess() {
8          if (conversation.isTransient()) {
9              conversation.begin();
10         }
11     }
12
13     public void addItemsOrder() {
14
15     }
16
17     public void endOrderProcess() {
18         if (!conversation.isTransient()) {
19             conversation.end();
20         }
21     }
22 }
```

In the code above, we have a bean called OrderService that is annotated @ConversationScoped on line 1. This bean also bears the serializable marker interface because it might get passivated by the container.

Line 4 uses the @Inject annotation to request for a contextual object of a bean type called Conversation, line 5. This is the first time we are using the @Inject annotation. It's the magic wand for requesting for contextual instances from the CDI container. The annotated bean type Conversation is a CDI bean that the container provides for us. It's not part of our developer code.

The Conversation bean has methods that we use to check if a bean is transient or not, begin and end conversations, and get the ID of the current conversation. Line 7 defines a method called beginOrderProcess() that first checks if the current instance is in transient mode. If it is, then the method begin() is invoked on the injected Conversation instance.

Line 13 then defines a method called addItemsToOrder() that is responsible for adding items to the cart. This method can be implemented in any way depending on the issue at hand.

Line 17 finally declares a method called endConversation() that checks whether a bean is not transient, and proceeds to invoke the end() method on the injected Conversation object. Invoking the end() method makes the OrderService instance transient, ready to be have its context destroyed.

DEPENDENT PSEUDO-SCOPE[13]

@Dependent is a pseudo scope according to the CDI spec. It is the default scope a bean is scoped to when no explicit scopes are declared for it. Psuedo scoped beans have at least two important points that distinguish them from other scopes

- No injected instance of the bean is ever shared between multiple injection points.
- Any instance of the bean injected into an object that is being created by the container, is bound to the life cycle of the created object.

This implies every single request for a Dependent scoped bean results in a new instance and the life of that instance is bound to the life of its injection point. Generally, I would recommend you explicitly declare scopes for your beans as an application developer.

So far you have seen the various contexts that are provided to you out of the box by the CDI container. You have seen @ApplicationScoped, @RequestScoped, @SessionScoped and @ConversationScoped. However, one question we have not answered to this point, is where and how can we make a request for contextual instances? We have seen how to create our own CDI beans, but how do we use them? How do we put the CDI container to our service?

CDI INJECTION POINTS

There are three main injection points where you can use the @Inject annotation to request for contextual instances from the CDI container.

FIELD INJECTION POINT

We saw our first injection point when we looked at the OrderService class earlier, reproduced below.

```
1  @ConversationScoped
2  public class OrderService implements Serializable {
3
4      @Inject
5      Conversation conversation;
6
7      public void beginOrderProcess() {
8          if (conversation.isTransient()) {
9              conversation.begin();
10         }
11     }
12
13     public void addItemsOrder() {
14
15     }
16
17     public void endOrderProcess() {
18         if (!conversation.isTransient()) {
19             conversation.end();
20         }
21     }
22 }
```

Line 4 uses the @Inject annotation on bean type Conversation. This is a field injection point where we are requesting the CDI container create a contextual instance of the Conversation bean and inject it into the provided variable of that type. Field injection is by far the most popular, and in my view, intuitive way of requesting for dependencies.

METHOD INJECTION

Method injection is when a method is annotated with @Inject annotation with one or more parameters. These methods are called initializer methods and will be invoked automatically by the container. All parameters of a method injection point must be valid CDI beans.

CONSTRUCTOR INJECTION

Constructor injection is when we annotate a bean constructor with the @Inject annotation with one or more parameters. All parameters will be resolved by the container. Only one constructor injection is allowed per CDI bean.

```
1  @RequestScoped
2  public class SearchService {
3
4      private final Collection<Order> searchResults = new HashSet<>();
5
6      QueryService queryService;
7
8      @Inject
9      public SearchService(QueryService qS) {
10         this.queryService = qS;
11     }
12
13     public Collection<Order> searchOrders(String reqQueryString, String... optionalQueryStrings) {
14         //perform search in datastore and put results in searchResults
15
16         return searchResults;
17     }
18 }
19
```

In the above modified SearchService bean, line 6 declares a field of type QueryService, which is itself a bean. Line 8 uses @Inject on the constructor declaration (line 9) to inject an instance of QueryService into the parameter. We then use this injected parameter to initialize the QueryService field declared in line 6. There are other injection points as well, found in producer methods and observer methods, which we will be looking at a little later in this chapter.

You now seen CDI beans, the various scopes you can assign their contextual instances to, and points that you can request for those contextual instances. CDI however, has two broad kinds of beans. What we have looked at so far are called managed beans. The other kind of beans is session beans, not to be confused with session contexts.

KINDS OF CDI BEANS

MANAGED BEANS

Managed beans are what you have seen so far in this book. They are Java classes that have either explicit CDI annotations for beans that have the bean-discovery-mode of the beans.xml file set to annotated, or implicit for beans that have the bean-discovery-mode set to all. In addition, a bean is a managed bean if

- It is not a non-static inner class.
- It is a concrete class or is annotated with @Decorator.
- It has an appropriate constructor - either:
  o   The class has a constructor with no parameters, or
  o   The class declares a constructor annotated with @Inject.

For a given managed bean like

```java
1 @RequestScoped
2 public class SearchService {
3
4
5     private final Collection<Order> searchResults = new HashSet<>();
6     public Collection<Order> searchOrders(String reqQueryString, String... optionalQueryStrings) {
7         //perform search in datastore and put results in searchResults
8
9         return searchResults;
10    }
11 }
12
```

Its set of bean types are

- All super classes up to java.lang.Object
- All implemented interfaces, directly or indirectly and
- The bean class itself

SESSION BEANS

Session beans are Java classes annotated with meta
data from the Enterprise JavaBeans[14] spec. Technically, local Stateless, Stateful and Singleton EJBs
are automatically CDI beans that support the various CDI services like injection, interception and
scoping. Using EJBs in a CDI application makes the features of both specs available to you.

Creating session bean is quite simple as seen in the code below.

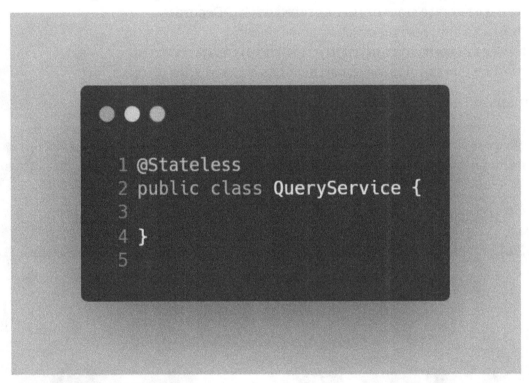

```
1 @Stateless
2 public class QueryService {
3
4 }
5
```

In this code, we have our QueryService class annotated with @Stateless. This makes the bean both
a CDI managed bean and a Stateless EJB. We can inject instances of this bean anywhere we can inject
a managed bean. The EJB spec aims at making development of business component easy and almost
effortless.

The @Stateless annotation on the QueryService above transforms it into a class that has transactional methods by default, is pooled, secured and other helpful features that you would have had to
worry about. Do take a look at the EJB spec for more information about the power of that API.

The bean type of a session bean are
> • All super classes up to java.lang.Object
> • All implemented interfaces, directly or indirectly (for beans with local interfaces) and
> • The bean class itself

CDI QUALIFIERS

You have so far seen almost all there is to know about CDI beans. However, you might be wondering what happens if two or more beans implement the same interface and you want to inject using the given interface. To use our restaurant application, let's say we have an interface, of type GenericOrder that has one method, order() as shown below.

```java
1 public interface GenericOrder {
2
3     BigDecimal order();
4 }
```

This interface has a method that returns the total of a given order. Let's say our restaurant has a website where a user can logon and place a self-service order to the kitchen for delivery. Patrons can also walk in and place orders that will be entered into the system by our restaurant attendants or cashiers.

We want to modify our @ConversationScoped OrderService bean to implement the GenericOrder instead of having its own order method. This is shown in the code below.

```java
1  @ConversationScoped
2  public class OrderService implements
3          GenericOrder, Serializable {
4
5      @Inject
6      Conversation conversation;
7
8      public void beginOrderProcess() {
9          if (conversation.isTransient()) {
10             conversation.begin();
11         }
12     }
13
14     @Override
15     public BigDecimal order() {
16         return null;
17     }
18
19     public void endOrderProcess() {
20         if (!conversation.isTransient()) {
21             conversation.end();
22         }
23     }
24
25
26 }
```

Line 15 implements the order() method of the GenericOrder interface. This OrderService will be used to service orders placed by patrons that physically walk into our restaurant to dine. We then want another service, SelfService that also implements GenericOrder to service online clients.

The code below shows the SelfService implementation

```java
1 @ConversationScoped
2 public class SelfService implements
3         GenericOrder, Serializable {
4
5     @Inject
6     Conversation conversation;
7
8     public void beginOrderProcess() {
9         if (conversation.isTransient()) {
10            conversation.begin();
11        }
12    }
13
14    @Override
15    public BigDecimal order() {
16        return null;
17    }
18
19    public void endOrderProcess() {
20        if (!conversation.isTransient()) {
21            conversation.end();
22        }
23    }
24
25 }
```

The SelfService implementation is identical to the OrderService implementation, for now. We are separating the two implementations right from now because in the future, clients that place their orders online will be treated completely differently, in terms of pricing, reward schemes, raffles and other incentives that we intend to introduce. So it's good practice to separate the two implementations now instead of having to refactor or introduce a new implementation after our application has become very complex.

So now we have two classes that implement the same interface. Trying to do an @Inject by the GenericOrder interface as shown below will fail.

```
1 @RequestScoped
2 public class OrderFacade {
3
4     @Inject
5     GenericOrder genericOrder;
6 }
```

In the code above, we have a CDI bean named OrderFacade that is request scoped. This bean has a field injection of type GenericOrder on line 5. This code will compile fine but will fail deployment. The CDI container, remember, validates our archive to ensure we are in line with the requirements of the CDI spec.

The above code will fail CDI container validation with a message that the injection point GenericOrder is ambiguous. We have more than one class implementing the GenericOrder interface and are requesting for a contextual instance through the interface. The container will not know which concrete bean type we want.

You will encounter these kinds of issues in your own code. To prevent these kind of ambiguous dependency issues, the CDI spec give you the concept of Qualifiers. They are annotations that we create, place them on beans that we want to identify with such annotations, and then annotate injection points if we want injection points resolved to the annotated bean type. It all sounds more complex than it is. So let's create two Qualifiers for our order services - an OnlineQualifier and InStoreQualifier.

```
1 @Qualifier
2 @Retention(RUNTIME)
3 @Target({FIELD, TYPE, METHOD, PARAMETER})
4 public @interface OnlineQualifier {
5
6 }
```

In the above code, we have an annotation declaration on line 4 with the name OnlineQualifier. This annotation is annotated with the @Qualifier annotation which tells the CDI container that we want to have our OnlineQualifier annotation regarded as a CDI qualifier.

Lines 2 and 3 of the code sets the retention and targets of the OnlineQualifier annotation. This is pretty much all we need to declare our annotation. We will use the same constructs for the InStore-Qualifier as shown below.

```
1 @Qualifier
2 @Retention(RUNTIME)
3 @Target({FIELD, TYPE, METHOD, PARAMETER})
4 public @interface InStoreQualifier {
5
6 }
7
```

So, with our annotations declared, we now need to associate them with the respective beans we want to use them for. We will use the OnlineQualifier to qualify our SelfService bean, and the InStoreQualifier for the OrderService beans. The respective code samples are reproduced below.

```
1  @ConversationScoped
2  @OnlineQualifier
3  public class SelfService implements
4          GenericOrder, Serializable {
5
6      @Inject
7      Conversation conversation;
8
9      public void beginOrderProcess() {
10         if (conversation.isTransient()) {
11             conversation.begin();
12         }
13     }
14
15     @Override
16     public BigDecimal order() {
17         return null;
18     }
19
20     public void endOrderProcess() {
21         if (!conversation.isTransient()) {
22             conversation.end();
23         }
24     }
25
26 }
```

The OnlineQualifier is associated with the SelfService bean on line 2 of the above code.

```java
1 @ConversationScoped
2 @InStoreQualifier
3 public class OrderService implements
4         GenericOrder, Serializable {
5
6     @Inject
7     Conversation conversation;
8
9     public void beginOrderProcess() {
10         if (conversation.isTransient()) {
11             conversation.begin();
12         }
13     }
14
15     @Override
16     public BigDecimal order() {
17         return null;
18     }
19
20     public void endOrderProcess() {
21         if (!conversation.isTransient()) {
22             conversation.end();
23         }
24     }
25
26
27 }
```

The InStoreQualifier is now associated with the OrderService bean on line 2. So now we have two beans of the type GenericOrder but both having separate qualifiers. With the above in place, we now go back to the OrderFacade bean and qualify the GenericOrder injection point.

```
1 @RequestScoped
2 public class OrderFacade {
3     @Inject
4     @InStoreQualifier
5     GenericOrder genericOrder;
6 }
7
```

Line 4 uses the @InStoreQualifier to tell the container to resolve the GenericOrder type to the OrderService concrete type. This way, even though you request for instances through a common interface implemented by more than one class, there is no ambiguity with regards to type resolution.

You can, in the same class, inject another GenericOrder field and qualify it with the OnlineQualifier as shown below.

```
1 @RequestScoped
2 public class OrderFacade {
3     @Inject
4     @InStoreQualifier
5     GenericOrder genericOrder;
6
7     @Inject
8     @OnlineQualifier
9     GenericOrder onlineOrder;
10 }
```

As you can see, there are two field injection points in the OrderFace bean now, all using the GenericOrder interface but both qualified with their respective concrete type qualifiers.

This is how you can use Qualifiers to prevent ambiguity in your code, while at the same time improving the readability and extensibility of it. Qualifiers can be used for much more powerful tasks, though, as we will see in the Events section of this chapter.

BUILT-IN QUALIFIERS

Aside from the ability to create your own CDI Qualifiers, the CDI API also does come with some built in Qualifiers out of the box. These are

@Any[15] - This is a qualifier added to all beans by default, even if the bean doesn't declare any qualifiers.

@Named[16] - This is a string based qualifier used to make intances of the annotated bean available for reference in a weakly typed environment, like a JSF page or JavaScript.

@Default[17] - This qualifier is used automatically where a bean doesn't explicitly declare a qualify aside from @Named.

@Initialized[18] - This qualifier is used to qualify an automatically fired event when a context is initialized and ready to use. We will talk about Events later in this chapter.

@Destroyed[19] - This qualifier is used to qualify an automatically fired event when a context is destroyed.

Right to this point, you have covered quite a lot of CDI stuff, enough to make you capable of writing better. However, there's even more to learn, so let's go on and take a look at the concept of CDI producers, what they are and how you can use them.

CDI PRODUCERS

Producers in CDI are an API construct that you can use to turn beans or classes you don't own into CDI managed beans, complete with qualifiers and scopes. Let's go back to our restaurant app. We want to have the username of the currently executing user at any time. There are two ways we can achieve that.

The first is to simply @Inject the UserSession bean and invoke the getUserName() method on the instance. The second, more extensible way, would be to create a producer method of type String that returns the username. This way, we can @Inject into a field of type String and the container will know where to get what we want. You can sweeten things by qualifying your producer methods.

METHOD PRODUCERS

It's quite simple than words make it, so let's look at our first producer method that returns the currently executing username.

```java
 1 public class MyProducer {
 2
 3     @Inject
 4     UserSession userSession;
 5
 6     @Produces
 7     public String produceUserName() {
 8         return userSession.getUserName();
 9     }
10 }
```

In the code above, we have a bean named MyProducer (for lack of imagination on my part), that has an injected field of type UserSession on line 4. Line 7 declares a method called produceUserName() that returns a String type. This method is annotated with @Produces[20] on line 6. This annotation transforms this method into a CDI producer that will be consulted for instances to satisfy String injection types.

You can then use the producer method to inject String types into your other components as shown below.

```
1 @RequestScoped
2 public class OrderFacade {
3
4     @Inject
5     String userName;
6
7     @Inject
8     @InStoreQualifier
9     GenericOrder genericOrder;
10
11     @Inject
12     @OnlineQualifier
13     GenericOrder onlineOrder;
14 }
```

Line 4 of the above code uses @Inject to request for an instance of type String into the userName field (line 5) of the OrderFacade bean. This should work fine assuming you don't use any third party code in your application.

If you do however, libraries such as OmniFaces[21], have producer methods that return String. In our restaurant app, we have the OmniFaces library as part of our application dependencies. So, the above String injection point will cause our code to fail container validation at application startup, even though it will compile just fine.

In this case, we can use a Qualifier to qualifier our producer method and injection point. Let's see the qualifier declaration below

```
1 @Qualifier
2 @Retention(RUNTIME)
3 @Target({FIELD, TYPE, METHOD, PARAMETER})
4 public @interface UserNameQualifier {
5
6 }
7
```

In the above code, we declare a qualifier called UserNameQualifier, which we associate with the producer method as shown below.

```
1 public class MyProducer {
2
3     @Inject
4     UserSession userSession;
5
6     @Produces
7     @UserNameQualifier
8     public String produceUserName() {
9         return userSession.getUserName();
10    }
11 }
```

Line 7 annotates the produceUserName() method with the @UserNameQualifier to ensure that we can distinguish our producer method from any other, whether in our own code or any third party library. Finally, we qualify the injection point with the same qualifier.

```java
1  @RequestScoped
2  public class OrderFacade {
3
4      @Inject
5      @UserNameQualifier
6      String userName;
7
8      @Inject
9      @InStoreQualifier
10     GenericOrder genericOrder;
11
12     @Inject
13     @OnlineQualifier
14     GenericOrder onlineOrder;
15 }
16
```

Line 5 annotates the userName field with @UserNameQualifier to tell the container to consult our annotated producer method for an instance to satisfy this injection point. This is how you can use producers methods in a nutshell.

What you have seen so far is what is called producer methods. We could scope the producer method return type to a specific scope instead of leaving it to the default @Dependent scope. But, there is a caveat, according to the CDI API, "if a producer method sometimes returns a null value, or if a producer field sometimes contains a null value when accessed, then the producer method or field must have scope @Dependent."

We could have a situation where our code requests for a userName when no user is logged in. In such a case, our producer method might return null, and thus we leave it to the default @Dependent scope. However, just know you can annotate your producer methods with a specific scope and returned types from the method will be put in that context.

PRODUCER FIELDS

Producer fields are similar to producer methods in that they both act as sources for contextual instances. Producer fields however, are just fields of a bean annotated with @Produces annotation. The annotated field can be equally qualified and scoped as can be done with a producer method. A typical use of producer fields is producing EntityManager[22] objects for JPA as shown below.

```
1 public class MyProducer {
2
3     @Produces
4     @PersistenceContext
5     EntityManager entityManager;
6
7 }
8
```

Line 5 declares field of type EntityManager, annotated with @PersistenceContext on line 4 and @Prouces on line 3. This is a classic case of field producers where we are using two annotations from two APIs to produce an object. The @PersistenceContext annotation is from the JPA and is used to link this EntityManager object to the persistence context. We then use the CDI @Produces annotation to make this field capable of satisfying JPA EntityManager injection points in our code.

CDI BEAN LIFECYCLE CALLBACKS

CDI beans, as has been discussed to this point, are managed by the container. All we have to do is request for instances from the container. However, there are times when we need to do some for initialization, or de-initialization of our beans before we use them.

A typical example could be when you need to fetch some form of list from the database for display in the UI before the UI access the bean. Another example is releasing system resources held in a bean before the bean is destroyed. You will encounter these a lot in your own applications.

The CDI API gives you annotations you can place on methods to transform those methods into automatically invoked lifecycle callbacks.

@POSTCONSTRUCT[23]

A method annotated @PostConstruct will be automatically invoked when a bean instance is fully constructed, all dependencies of the bean have been satisfied but just before the bean is put into service.

A method annotated @PostConstruct must not have a return type nor take any parameters, except for interceptors (we'll talk about them later), for which case they can take an InvocationContext[24] object. A @PostConstruct annotated method can be private, package private, protected or public.

In our code, we would want to pre-populate a list with the last 10 orders of a self-service user that logons to use our online portal. In our SelfService bean, as shown below, we can use the @PostConstruct callback method.

```
1 @ConversationScoped
2 @OnlineQualifier
3 public class SelfService implements
4         GenericOrder, Serializable {
5
6     List<Order> lastOrders = new ArrayList<>();
7
8     @PostConstruct
9     private void init() {
10        //Populate list from DB
11    }
12
13 }
```

Line 6 declares a Order typed List object. Line 8 declares method init() on line 9 as a callback method with the @PostConstruct annotation. The method signature is straightforward - returns void, named init (part of my naming convention) and is declared private. At runtime, the container will automatically invoke this method once all injection points in the bean have been satisfied but just before the bean is put into service.

@PREDESTROY[25]

This annotation can be used on a method that should be invoked just before a bean instance is destroyed by the container.

So far we've seen how all the of the various CDI API constructs work together. Next up, let's talk about the concept of CDI interceptors, what they are, what problem they solve and how you can create them.

CDI INTERCEPTORS

For every application, you will have situations where you need to dynamically perform tasks on bean invocations that are orthogonal to core function of those beans. A typical example is logging and security.

In our code for example, we would want to log method invocations on certain beans. We could manually implement the logging feature in all the beans we would want to log method invocations on. However, that would be implementing features in the beans that aren't really their core. Also because the logging feature is a cross-cutting concern, we should abstract that away from the beans. CDI interceptors can help us achieve that goal.

There are two parts to realizing interceptors using the CDI API. The first is to create an interceptor binding annotation. The second is to link the interceptor binding annotation to a bean that will implement the interceptor method. Let's first create our interceptor binding annotation in our restaurant app.

```
1 @Inherited
2 @Target({TYPE, METHOD})
3 @Retention(RUNTIME)
4 @InterceptorBinding
5 public @interface Logging {
6
7 }
8
```

Line 5 declares an annotation with the name Logging - you could name your interceptor binding annotation anything. Line 4 uses the @InterceptorBinding[26] annotation to declare that this annotation is an interceptor binding annotation. Note the target of the annotation is Type and Method, meaning we can use our interceptor for a whole class or just a method of that class. The @InterceptorBinding annotation is from the javax.interceptor package. Now let's implement the bean that will carry out the logic of the interceptor.

```
1  @Interceptor
2  @Logging
3  @Priority(Interceptor.Priority.APPLICATION)
4  public class LoggingBean {
5
6      @Inject
7      private Logger logger;
8
9      @AroundInvoke
10     public Object log(InvocationContext invocationContext) throws Exception {
11
12         //Log the invocation using whatever logging framework. We'll just use java.util.Logger
13         logger.log(Level.INFO, "Method " + invocationContext.getMethod().getName() + " invoked.");
14         return invocationContext.proceed();
15     }
16 }
```

Line 4 declares a class called LoggingBean annotated with @Interceptor on line 1. This annotation makes this class an interceptor bean. Line 2 annotates the same class with the @Logging interceptor annotation. This links our annotation to this class. This means anytime we annotate a method or class with our @Logging annotation, the CDI container will instantiate this class to carry our the logic of the interceptor.

Line 3 also annotates the class with @Priority annotation, taking a Interceptor.Priority.APPLICATION as parameter. Before Java EE 7, you need to activate interceptors through an XML config file. However, after version 7, you could use the @Priority annotation to activate and order/prioritize your interceptors. In this case, we are passing it the APPLICATION constant, which is just an int value.

Line 10 declares a method called log() that takes a single object of type InvocationContext[27], returns Object and throws Exception. This method is annotated @AroundInvoke on line 9. Method log() is the place we implement the logic of our interceptor, using an injected Logger - line 6 and 7 - to log the invoked method name. In this method, you can implement any logic that cuts across classes.

The InvocationContext object is a bean that gives you information about the - drumroll - context of the invocation for which this interceptor has been dispatched. It has methods you can use to get information about the method parameter if the interceptor was dispatched for a method, information about the constructor if this interceptor was dispatched for a class, get and set method parameters and a method to tell the container to proceed with the invocation of the next interceptor, or method if none.

Line 14 invokes the proceed() method on the InvocationContext. This tells the container to proceed to the next interceptor if more than one has been dispatched, or to the method call if this is the only interceptor.

Assuming you were implementing security instead of logging, and after doing some security checks, your code decides the currently executing user should not be invoking the target method for which this interceptor was dispatched, you can return null and the container will not proceed to invoke the target method.

With our interceptor implemented, all we have to do to use it is annotate a method we want to log in a given bean. Let's log method order invocations on our OrderService bean.

```java
1  @ConversationScoped
2  @InStoreQualifier
3  public class OrderService implements
4          GenericOrder, Serializable {
5
6      @Inject
7      Conversation conversation;
8
9      public void beginOrderProcess() {
10          if (conversation.isTransient()) {
11              conversation.begin();
12          }
13      }
14
15      @Override
16      @Logging
17      public BigDecimal order() {
18          return null;
19      }
20
21      public void endOrderProcess() {
22          if (!conversation.isTransient()) {
23              conversation.end();
24          }
25      }
26  }
```

Line 16 uses our @Logging annotation to log invocations of order() method on the OrderService bean. Every invocation of this method will cause the container to dispatch our interceptor. And since we ask for the invocation to proceed at the end of our interceptor logic implementation, invocation will proceed to method order() after logging.

This is how simple it is to implement interceptors using the CDI API. Create your interceptor binding annotation, then link that annotation to an interceptor bean with a method annotated with @AroundInvoke that implements your interceptor logic. To use your interceptor, annotate any method or class - depending on your interceptor annotation target - with your interceptor annotation. Next up, let's talk about CDI events, what they are, why you'd want to use them, how to create them and how to use them. Let's go.

CDI EVENTS

SYNCHRONOUS EVENTS

CDI events are an API construct that helps your application components communicate with each other without any form of compile time dependencies, or they even knowing about each other. It entails an event object of any valid Java type, optionally with qualifiers and one or more event listeners, also optionally with qualifiers.

The Event[28] object fires an event of its payload type, and the CDI container automatically invokes observers that are observing that particular event fired based on event payload type and optionally, qualifiers. In our restaurant application, we want to have feature where we send an SMS to a user who places on an order online to acknowledge our receipt of the order and to give them an ETA.

We could implement such a feature using events. First we need an Event object with a suitable payload, and an observer that observes that same payload event type. Let's see that in code.

```java
1  @ConversationScoped
2  @OnlineQualifier
3  public class SelfService implements
4          GenericOrder, Serializable {
5
6      @Inject
7      Event<ApplicationUser> messageEvent;
8
9      @Inject
10     UserSession userSession;
11
12     @Override
13     public BigDecimal order() {
14         //fire a message event to send SMS before returning from this method
15         messageEvent.fire(userSession.getCurrentUser());
16         return null;
17     }
18
19
20 }
21
```

We start by using @Inject to request a Event bean typed to ApplicationUser on line 7. The event interface is the starting point of the CDI event mechanism. The injected Event instance is then used to fire a ApplicationUser event in the order() method on line 15, using the fire(T event) method.

Because the Event bean is typed to a ApplicationUser object (line 7), the fire method used to fire the event must be passed an instance of the ApplicationUser class. This is the event payload, or data that will be passed to event observers, and in this case, also used to choose which observers to invoke for the event. We use the injected UserSession - lines 9 and 10 - in the SelfService class to get the currently executing user by invoking the getCurrentUser() method - line 15.

The ApplicationUser class is a bean that models an application user, as shown below.

```
1 public class ApplicationUser {
2
3     private String userName;
4     private String email;
5     private String address;
6     private String mobileNumber;
7     private String hashedPassword;
8 }
9
```

The updated UserSession bean is shown below.

```
1 @SessionScoped
2 public class UserSession implements Serializable {
3
4     private LocalDateTime loggedInTime;
5     private LocalDateTime loggedOutTime;
6
7     private ApplicationUser currentUser;
8
9     public ApplicationUser getCurrentUser() {
10        return currentUser;
11    }
12
13
14 }
15
```

The UserSession bean now has a field of type ApplicationUser on line 7. This is going to be set in one way or another by some kind of security layer, after a user successfully authenticates herself to the system. For now we'll just use it as it is.

With the event fired, you will need at least one observer to listen for that particular event. Because our event has no explicit qualifiers, the event observer will be selected based on the event payload type for which it is observing. Let's see our observer code.

```
1 public class MyEventListener {
2
3     void smsObserver(@Observes ApplicationUser applicationUser) {
4         try {
5             Thread.sleep(5000);
6             //Simulate sending SMS, which might be a long running task
7         } catch (InterruptedException e) {
8             e.printStackTrace();
9         }
10    }
11 }
12
```

The event observer is declare in a bean class of type MyEventListener. It has one method called smsObserver that takes one argument of type ApplicationUser. The only new CDI API in this method is the @Observes annotation. This annotation transforms this method into a CDI observer for event type ApplicationUser, as fired from the SelfService class.

At runtime, when an event is fired from the SelfService class, the container will cycle through all our event observers looking for events that observe the specific type fired. Once it comes across this method, it will invoke it and pass in the payload passed to the fire method of the event object.

In our observer, we simulate a long-running task of sending an SMS, which might take sometime because it has to do with network communication. Once the method returns, execution is returned to the point of fire and then continues on from there.

There are a few rules to declare an event observer -
The return type must be void
- It must have at least one parameter annotated with @Observes for event type to be observed
- Other parameters to the observer method must be CDI managed beans capable of injection
- The observer must be declared in a CDI bean.

As shown, firing and observing events with CDI is very easy and intuitive. As you might have noticed, the event observer has nothing to do with the SelfService class. The MyEventListener bean is oblivious of any bean that fires an event. You can have multiple event firing points for the same event type and each time your event observer will be invoked, without all components knowing about each other. This is compelling if you think about it.

ASYNC EVENTS

We can however, improve our event mechanism further in our restaurant application code. If you notice, the event observer in the MyEventListener class performs a blocking task. We would want to improve the responsiveness of our application by spawning long-running tasks to new threads. So instead of sending an SMS in the same thread that fired the event, we would want to do that in a different thread. Can we do that with the event mechanism of CDI? Yes of course. Let's see how, starting from the event firing side.

```java
1  @ConversationScoped
2  @OnlineQualifier
3  public class SelfService implements
4          GenericOrder, Serializable {
5
6      @Inject
7      Event<ApplicationUser> messageEvent;
8
9      @Override
10     public BigDecimal order() {
11
12         //fire a message event to send SMS before returning from this method
13 //        messageEvent.fire(userSession.getCurrentUser());
14         messageEvent.fireAsync(userSession.getCurrentUser());
15         return null;
16     }
17
18 }
```

In the code above, we use the same injected Event object - lines 7 and 8 - to fire an ApplicationUser event on line 14. The difference however, is that we invoked fireAsync method instead of the plain fire. This method fires an asynchronous event for all async observers to listen for it. Async events means control returns immediately. The observer method is executed simultaneously, or asynchronously. Let's see the async event observer implementation.

```
1 public class MyEventListener {
2
3     void smsAsyncObserver(@ObservesAsync ApplicationUser applicationUser) {
4         try {
5             Thread.sleep(5000);
6             //Simulate sending SMS, which might be a long running task
7             //You get the user phone number from ApplicationUser#getMobileNumber()
8
9         } catch (InterruptedException e) {
10            e.printStackTrace();
11        }
12    }
13 }
```

Line 3 declares a method, smsAsyncObserver that takes an ApplicationUser object as a parameter. The only new thing is the annotation we used for the parameter. Instead of @Observes as we did earlier, we are using @ObservesAsync. This is how you create an observer to listen to async events.

Because our code has only one asycn firing point and one asycn observer of the same payload type, this observer will be invoked. The best thing is that this observer will not block. Once it's invoked, execution will return to the order() method in the SelfService bean. This way, we can conveniently send our SMS without affecting the responsiveness of our application. This is how you implement async events in CDI. But there's more.

We can use Qualifiers to fire and observe events of the same type, but for different purposes. You can qualify the event object at injection point and the observer at the declaration point. The container will then link the observer to the event based on the qualifier. It's effortless to implement.

QUALIFYING EVENTS

Let's say in our application, we decide to send an SMS to all clients, whether self service or in-person diners. However, we'd want to have different message content for the two classes of clients. To do that, we'd want to qualify our events and observers with requisite qualifiers.

```java
1  @ConversationScoped
2  @OnlineQualifier
3  public class SelfService implements
4          GenericOrder, Serializable {
5
6      @Inject
7      @OnlineQualifier
8      Event<ApplicationUser> messageEvent;
9
10     @Override
11     public BigDecimal order() {
12
13         //fire a message event to send SMS before returning from this method
14 //        messageEvent.fire(userSession.getCurrentUser());
15         messageEvent.fireAsync(userSession.getCurrentUser());
16         return null;
17     }
18 }
19
```

The code above has only one change. On line 7, we use our @OnlineQualifier to qualify the injected event object. This marks this event as qualified and will only be listened to by observers with the same qualifier. Let's look at the observer.

```
1 public class MyEventListener {
2
3    void smsAsyncObserver(@ObservesAsync @OnlineQualifier ApplicationUser applicationUser) {
4        try {
5            Thread.sleep(5000);
6            //Simulate sending SMS, which might be a long running task
7            //You get the user phone number from ApplicationUser#getMobileNumber()
8
9        } catch (InterruptedException e) {
10            e.printStackTrace();
11        }
12    }
13 }
14
```

The above async observer is the same as before except for the method parameter on line 3 where we annotate the ApplicationUser with @OnlineQualifier. This single annotation links this observer to the event in SelfService. So we can now fire an async event in the SelfService class and have this observer invoked. However, all of this is quite useless if we have just one event firing point and one observer. The power of qualifying events comes to play when you have more than one event. Let's see that.

```
1 @ConversationScoped
2 @InStoreQualifier
3 public class OrderService implements
4        GenericOrder, Serializable {
5
6    @Inject
7    @InStoreQualifier
8    Event<ApplicationUser> messageEvent;
9
10    @Inject
11    UserSession userSession;
12
13
14    @Override
15    @Logging
16    public BigDecimal order() {
17
18        messageEvent.fireAsync(userSession.getCurrentUser());
19        return null;
20    }
21 }
22
```

The code above shows our OrderService bean, with two new fields - Event and UserSession. The event object on line 8 is qualified with the @InStoreQualifier on line 7. We then fire an async event on line 18 after an order is placed by a diner. This fired event can only be observed by @InStore-Qualifier qualified observers. So let's see that.

```
1  public class MyEventListener {
2
3      void smsInStore(@ObservesAsync @InStoreQualifier ApplicationUser applicationUser) {
4          try {
5              Thread.sleep(5000);
6              //Simulate sending SMS, which might be a long running task
7              //You get the user phone number from ApplicationUser#getMobileNumber()
8
9          } catch (InterruptedException e) {
10             e.printStackTrace();
11         }
12     }
13 }
14
```

In the above code, we declare an observer on line 3 called smsInStore with one parameter type - ApplicationUser. This parameter is annotated @ObservesAsynch and @InStoreQualifier, effectively making this observer responsible for the event fired from our OrderService class. This is how you can combine the various CDI API constructs to create very powerful applications, all the while keeping your code easy to read and maintainable.

TRANSACTIONAL EVENT OBSERVERS

All the event observers will be called when the event is fired. There are times, however, when you would like an event observer to be called at a specific time during a transaction. As an example, we have an ApplicationUser class in our application. We would like to send a welcome email to a self-service user that gets successfully registered with the application. However, we would only want to send the email if the user successfully get persisted in our datastore, or more technically, when the transaction completes successfully.

To do that, we create a new Qualifier, CreateUserQualifier, fire an event, declare a transactional observer that only gets called the transaction completes successfully. Let's start with the qualifier.

```
1 @Qualifier
2 @Retention(RUNTIME)
3 @Target({FIELD, TYPE, METHOD, PARAMETER})
4 public @interface CreateUserQualifier {
5
6 }
7
```

Line 4 shows an annotation declaration with name CreateUserQualifier, with requisite qualifier metadata declared on lines 1-3.

```
1 @Stateless
2 public class PersistenceService {
3
4     @Inject
5     @CreateUserQualifier
6     Event<ApplicationUser> emailEvent;
7
8     public ApplicationUser persistUser(ApplicationUser applicationUser) {
9         //Persist new user into datastore, returning the persisted user.
10        emailEvent.fire(applicationUser);
11
12        return applicationUser;
13
14    }
15 }
```

Line 2 of the above code declares PersistenceService bean which is set as a stateless EJB - line 1. We inject an event object on line 6, qualified on line 5 with @CreateUserQualifier. The class then declares a method called persistUser on line 8 that takes an ApplicationUser object as the parameter. In this method, you'd store the user in the datastore using some form of data API. We then fire an event on line 10 with the ApplicationUser object as the payload.

Because method persistUser is declared in an EJB, it will be executed in a transactional context. So we know that the event is being fired in a transactional context. Let's take a look at the observer for this event.

```
1 public class MyEventListener {
2
3     void sendEmail(@Observes(during = TransactionPhase.AFTER_SUCCESS)
4                    @CreateUserQualifier ApplicationUser applicationUser) {
5         //Send email using MessagingService
6     }
7 }
8
```

Line 3 declares an observer called sendEmail that takes an ApplicationUser as the payload. It's qualified with @CreateUserQualifier, and annotated @Observes. This time however, the @Observes annotation has a value set for the *during* parameter. This value of the during field of the @Observes annotation can be set to any of the following

- **TransactionPhase.IN_PROGRESS** - The event observer is invoked when the event is fired, without regard to the transaction phase. This is the default value for all the @Observes for we've seen so far.

- **TransactionPhase.BEFORE_COMPLETION** - The event observer is called during the before completion phase of the transaction.
- **TransactionPhase.BEFORE_COMPLETION** - The event observer is called during the after completion phase of the transaction.
- **TransactionPhase.AFTER_FAILURE** - The event observer is called during the after completion phase of the transaction but only if the transaction failed.
- **TransactionPhase.AFTER_SUCCESS** - The event observer is called during the after completion phase of the transaction but only if the transaction completed successfully.

The last value is what we used in our observer declaration. What we want is for this observer to be invoked only if the transaction in which we are persisting the new user completes successfully, in which case we know for certain the user has been persisted in our datastore. There's no point in sending a welcome email to a user that hasn't been successfully registered in the system.

Whew! What a ride. We have covered all that you will need to know to use the CDI API in your own code. It's impossible to cover everything about any given library in a book. However, with what you have learned to this point, you should a solid foundation on which you can explore the CDI spec[29] on your own.

If you need further help with any of the topics covered in this book, or would like me to help you out with a project, or simply hangout for coffee, please don't hesitate to reach out to me. I would love to hear from you and will respond to all your mails.

Thank you for reading this book. I appreciate your custom.

About the author

Hello there! Thanks for picking up this book. My name is Luqman, a Jakarta EE developer with Pedantic Devs. I have been doing software development for close to a decade. I started with PHP and now do Jakarta EE full time.

My goal is to help you get productive with the powerful, modern, intuitive and easy to use Jakarta EE APIs.

I'll serve you the best of vanilla, pure and awesome Jakarta EE books to help you master the skills needed to solve whatever development challenge you have at hand.

So check out my books and let's get started making you a Jakarta EE ninja.

---

[1] https://jcp.org/en/eg/eghome

[2] https://jcp.org/en/home/index

[3] https://en.wikipedia.org/wiki/Technology_Compatibility_Kit

[4] https://javaee.github.io/tutorial/

[5] https://en.wikipedia.org/wiki/Rod_Johnson_(programmer)

[6] **Why I Hate Spring** - http://samatkinson.com/why-i-hate-spring/

[7] https://en.wikipedia.org/wiki/Inversion_of_control

[8] http://docs.jboss.org/cdi/spec/2.0/cdi-spec.html#concepts

[9] https://docs.jboss.org/cdi/api/2.0/javax/enterprise/context/ApplicationScoped.html

[10] https://docs.jboss.org/cdi/api/2.0/javax/enterprise/context/RequestScoped.html

[11] https://docs.jboss.org/cdi/api/2.0/javax/enterprise/context/SessionScoped.html

[12] https://docs.jboss.org/cdi/api/2.0/javax/enterprise/context/ConversationScoped.html

[13] https://docs.jboss.org/cdi/api/2.0/javax/enterprise/context/Dependent.html

[14] https://download.oracle.com/otndocs/jcp/ejb-3_2-fr-spec/index.html

[15] https://docs.jboss.org/cdi/api/2.0/javax/enterprise/inject/Any.html

[16] https://docs.oracle.com/javaee/7/api/javax/inject/Named.html

[17] https://docs.jboss.org/cdi/api/2.0/javax/enterprise/inject/Default.html

[18] https://docs.jboss.org/cdi/api/2.0/javax/enterprise/context/Initialized.html

[19] https://docs.jboss.org/cdi/api/2.0/javax/enterprise/context/Destroyed.html

[20] https://docs.jboss.org/cdi/api/2.0/javax/enterprise/inject/Produces.html

[21] http://omnifaces.org/

[22] https://docs.oracle.com/javaee/7/api/javax/persistence/EntityManager.html

[23] https://docs.oracle.com/javaee/7/api/javax/annotation/PostConstruct.html

[24] https://docs.oracle.com/javaee/7/api/javax/interceptor/InvocationContext.html

[25] https://docs.oracle.com/javaee/7/api/javax/annotation/PreDestroy.html

[26] https://docs.oracle.com/javaee/7/api/javax/interceptor/InterceptorBinding.html

[27] https://docs.oracle.com/javaee/7/api/javax/interceptor/InvocationContext.html

[28] https://docs.jboss.org/cdi/api/2.0/javax/enterprise/event/Event.html

[29] http://docs.jboss.org/cdi/spec/2.0/cdi-spec.pdf

www.ingramcontent.com/pod-product-compliance
Lightning Source LLC
Chambersburg PA
CBHW080602060326
40689CB00021B/4907